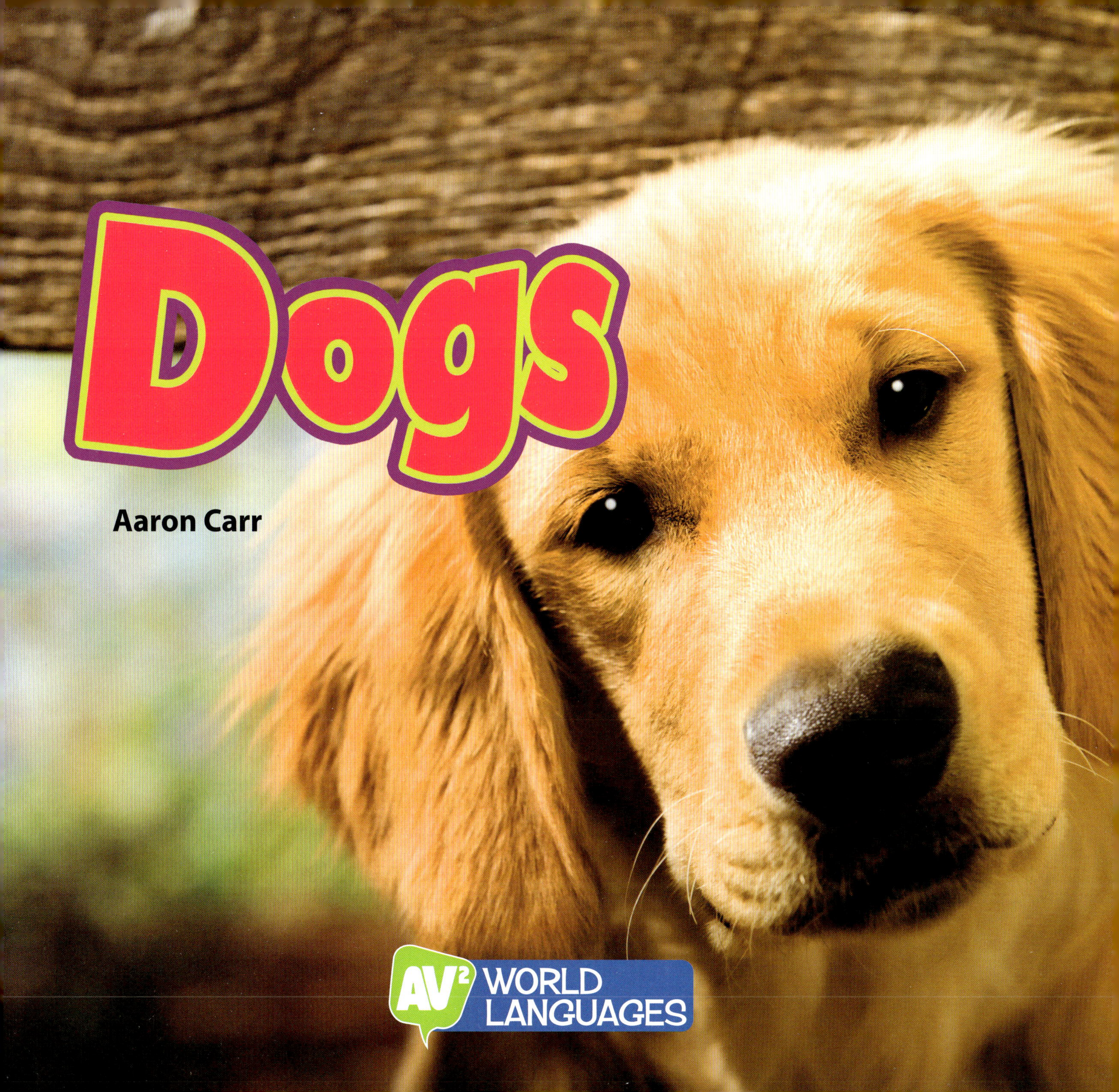
Dogs
Aaron Carr
AV2 WORLD LANGUAGES

AV2 WORLD LANGUAGES

Go to **openlightbox.com**, and enter the book's unique code.

BOOK CODE

AVU29938

Toggle between your **14 books in 14 languages.**

Easily move through highly visual pages.

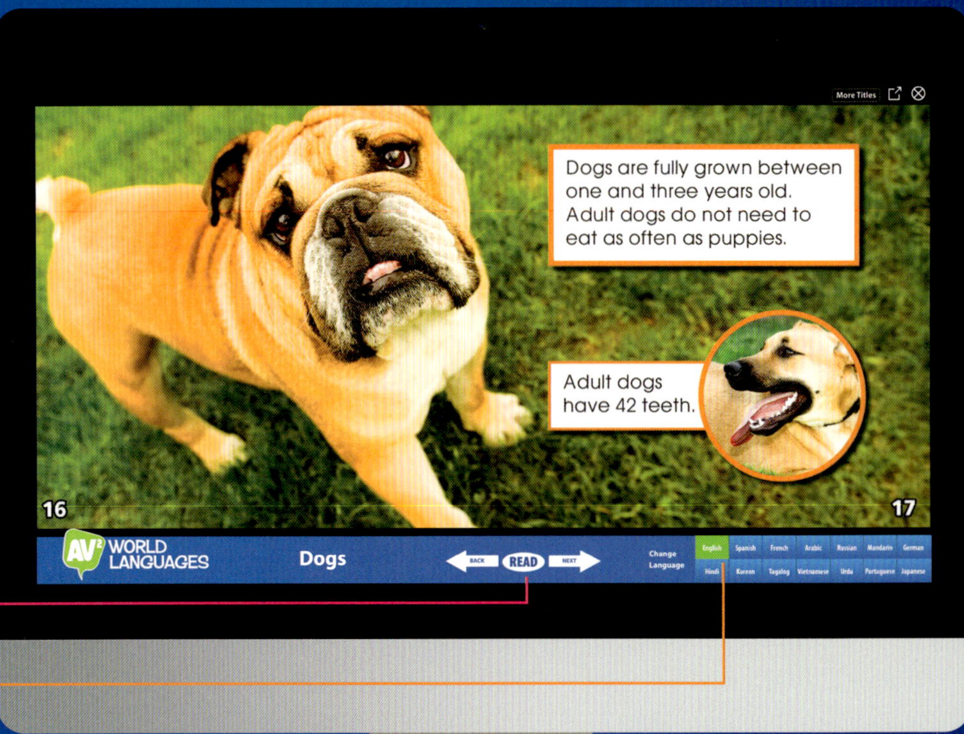

This title is part of our AV2 World Languages digital subscription.

Published by Lightbox Learning Inc.
276 5th Avenue, Suite 704 #917
New York, NY 10001
Website: www.openlightbox.com

Library of Congress Control Number: 2022931286

ISBN 978-1-7911-4581-1 (hardcover)
ISBN 978-1-7911-4582-8 (multi-user eBook)

Printed in Guangzhou, China
1 2 3 4 5 6 7 8 9 0 26 25 24 23 22

022022
102321

Project Coordinator: Jared Siemens
Art Director: Terry Paulhus

The publisher acknowledges Getty Images and iStock as its primary image suppliers for this title.

Dogs

CONTENTS

All animals begin life, grow, and have babies. The baby animals grow and become parents as well. This is called a life cycle.

Dogs are mammals. Mammals are warm-blooded animals. They can make their own body heat. Most mammals have hair or fur.

Dogs give birth to live babies. The babies can not see or hear for the first two weeks of their lives. Newborn puppies stay close together to keep warm.

Puppies drink their mother's milk.

Puppies begin to walk when they are about four weeks old.

Puppies grow baby teeth around four weeks old. They stop drinking milk and start to eat solid food at this time.

Puppies need to eat three or four times a day.

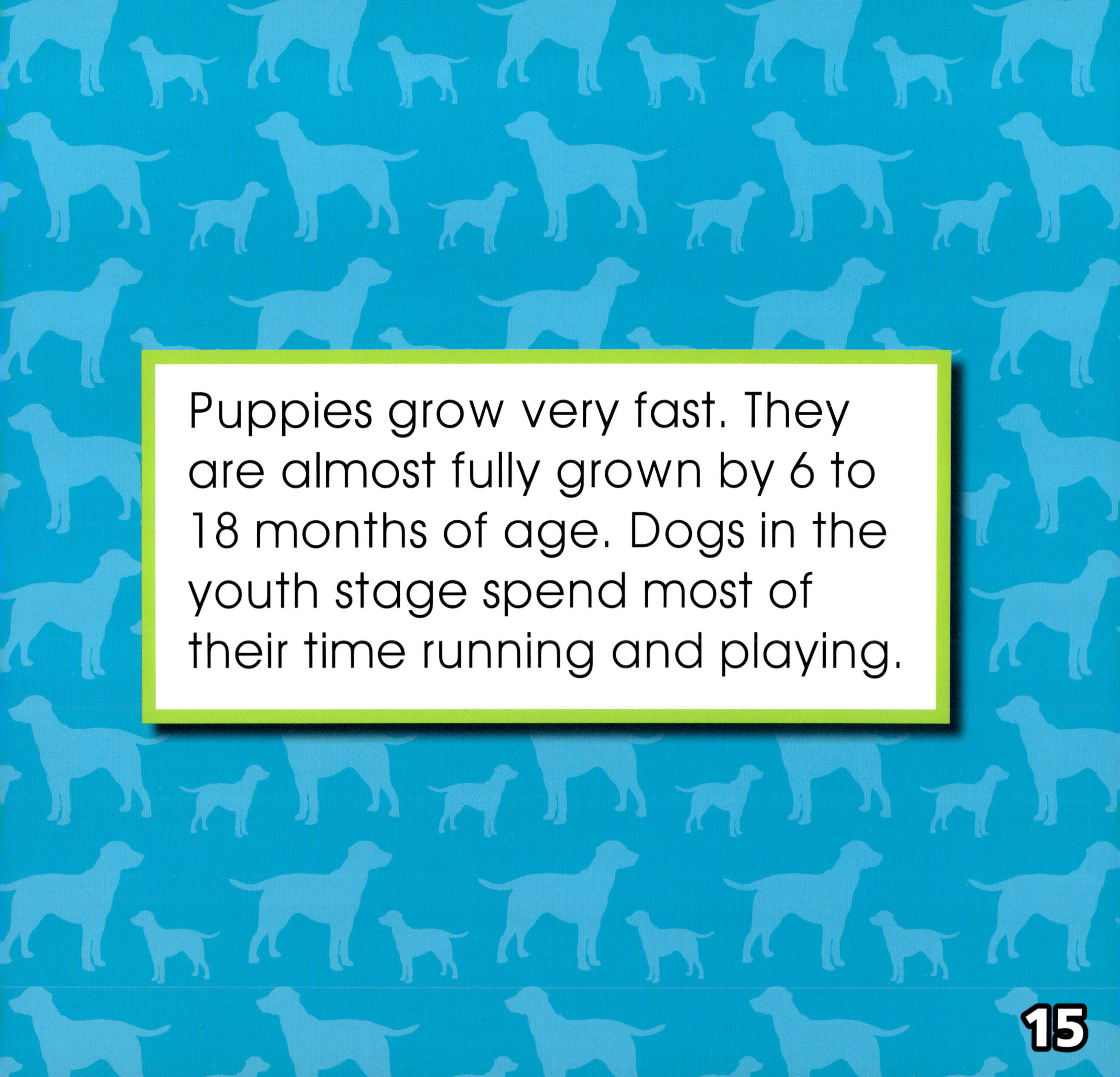

Puppies grow very fast. They are almost fully grown by 6 to 18 months of age. Dogs in the youth stage spend most of their time running and playing.

Dogs are fully grown between one and three years old. Adult dogs do not need to eat as often as puppies.

Adult dogs have 42 teeth.

Most dogs can have babies by one year of age. They carry their babies for nine weeks.

Dogs can give birth to 12 puppies at one time. This group of puppies is called a litter.

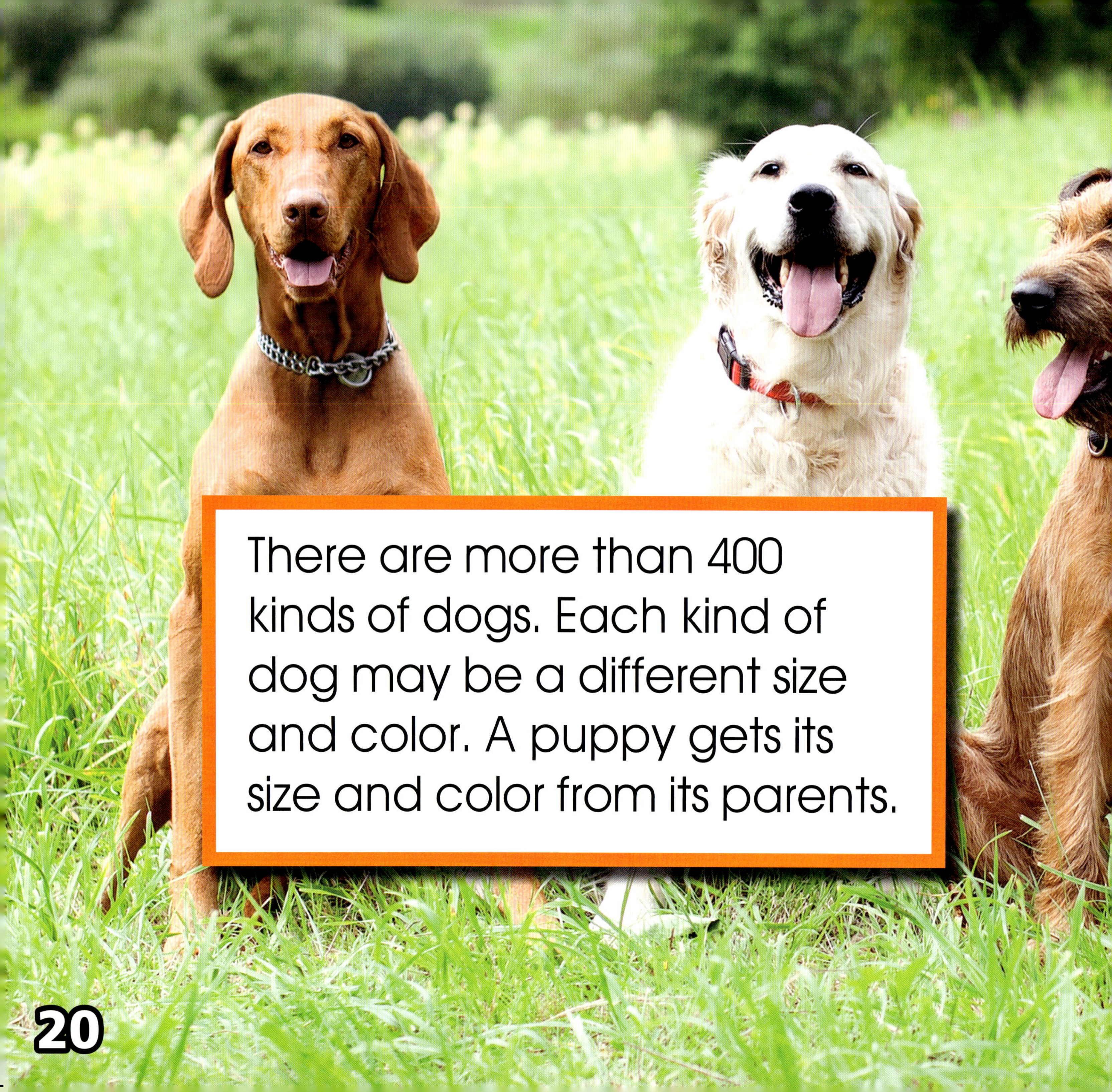

There are more than 400 kinds of dogs. Each kind of dog may be a different size and color. A puppy gets its size and color from its parents.

Life Cycles Quiz

Test your knowledge of dog life cycles by taking this quiz. Look at these pictures. Which stage of the life cycle do you see in each picture?

Newborn Puppy
Youth Adult

KEY WORDS

Research has shown that as much as 65 percent of all written material published in English is made up of 300 words. These 300 words cannot be taught using pictures or learned by sounding them out. They must be recognized by sight. This book contains 72 common sight words to help young readers improve their reading fluency and comprehension. This book also teaches young readers several important content words, such as proper nouns. These words are paired with pictures to aid in learning and improve understanding.

Page	Sight Words First Appearance
5	a, all, and, animals, as, begin, grow, have, is, life, the, this, well
7	are, can, make, most, or, own, their, they
8	close, first, for, give, hear, keep, live, mother, not, of, see, to, together, two
11	about, four, old, walk, when
12	around, at, day, eat, food, need, start, stop, three, time
15	almost, by, in, very
17	between, do, often, one, years
19	carry, group
20	be, each, different, from, gets, its, kinds, may, more, than, there

Page	Content Words First Appearance
5	babies, life cycle, parents
7	body, dogs, fur, hair, heat, mammals
8	birth, milk, puppies, weeks
12	teeth
15	age, months, stage, youth
19	litter
20	color, size